The Best of
DEMING

collected by
RON McCoy

INTRODUCTION

This book began in 1986 when I attended my first Four Day Seminar. I have been blessed with Dr. Deming's friendship. In 1987, I made a promise to my friend. At the conclusion of his first visit to my plant in Sioux City, Iowa, Dr. Deming said, "I will continue to work with you, if you are willing to share what you have learned."

The quotes are not written in the order that I collected them, nor are they categorized by topic. Each page has one quote to provide space for notes and questions. We learn in different ways. This little book is, for me, a fun way to learn. I write this book to keep my promise.

Ron McCoy

*You cannot hear
what you do not understand.*

We are here for an education.

Off we go ...
to the Milky Way!

You should not ask questions
without knowledge.

Information is not knowledge.
Let's not confuse the two.

There is no knowledge
without theory.

We do not know what quality is.

Our customers should take joy in our products and services.

Competition should not be for a share of the market— but to expand the market.

*We must satisfy
our customers.*

Management of outcomes may not be any more than a skill.
It does not require knowledge.

There must be consistency in direction.

What makes a scientist great is the care that he takes in telling you what is wrong with his results, so that you will not misuse them.

*If people did not make mistakes,
there would be no mistakes.*

*Experience teaches nothing
without theory.*

*3% of the problems
have figures,
97% of the problems do not.*

You do not install knowledge.

You cannot define
being exactly on time.

A rule should suit
the purpose.

Why aren't there enough napkins in the world? Is it a matter of distribution?

Work to the optimum.
When you depart a little,
*   there is a little loss.*
Depart further,
*   suffer more loss.*

By what method?
Use the one that corresponds
closest to your need.

We must understand variation.

*Anybody can predict
anything.*

Management does not know what a system is.

Have you ever known a golfer who was happy?

Without theory
we can only copy.

Quality is for the customer.

*We should be guided by theory,
not by numbers.*

Are you in favor of quality?

*Precise optimization
is not necessary.
It would be too costly.*

Shrink, shrink variation—
to reduce the loss.

*Understanding variation
is the key to success
in quality and business.*

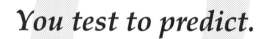

You test to predict.

You should not tamper with the process.

*If you do not know how to
ask the right question,
you discover nothing.*

*You cannot achieve an aim
unless you have a method.*

*If someone can make
a contribution to the company,
he feels important.*

*You do not find knowledge
in a dictionary,
only information.*

Deming's First Theorem:
"Nobody gives a hoot
about profits."

Deming's Second Theorem:
"We are being ruined
by best efforts."

We are here
to make another world.

People need to know how their job contributes.

*The merit system will put
us out of business.*

The emphasis should be on why we do a job.

*A leader's job
is to help his people.*

Retroactive management emphasizes the bottom line.

Management's job is to optimize the whole system.

Service is important.

*Judging people
does not help them.*

Management is prediction.

A leader
must have knowledge.
A leader
must be able to teach.

*When people try to do
what they cannot do,
they wish to give up.*

Making two people responsible guarantees mistakes.

*Managing by results
only makes things worse.*

Let us ask our suppliers
to come and help us
to solve our problems.

We want best efforts guided by theory.

Rational behavior requires theory. Reactive behavior requires only reflex action.

When we cooperate,
everybody wins.

There is no such thing as a fact.

*When a system is stable,
telling the worker about
mistakes is only tampering.*

*It does not happen
all at once.
There is no instant pudding.*

*Change the rule
and you will get
a new number.*

Ranking.
What good does it do?

Forces of Destruction:
grades in school,
merit system,
incentive pay,
business plans,
quotas.

*Innovation comes
from the producer—
not from the customer.*

*An integral part of the
theory of profound knowledge
is the operation of a system.*

*Confusing common causes
with special causes will
only make things worse.*

Confusing special and common causes are the greatest two mistakes.

Is price the price tag
or the total cost?

*You don't select leaders;
you select managers.*

*Meeting specifications
is not enough.*

You cannot inspect quality into the product; it is already there.

*When a worker has reached
a stable state,
further training will not
help him.*

*If a worker reaches
a stable state,
do not tell him about a mistake
unless it has a special cause.*

*A man that knows his limitations
is one that you can trust.*

*Plants don't close
from poor workmanship,
but from poor management.*

*A leader is obligated
to make changes
in the system of management.*

Why can't people work with pride?

Innovation comes from people who take joy in their work.

*It is not necessary
to confess past sins.*

Whenever there is fear,
you will get wrong figures.

The performance of any individual is to be judged in terms of his contribution to the aim of the system, not on his individual performance.

The main difference between service and manufacturing is the service department doesn't know that they have a product.

*Sub-optimization
is when everyone is for himself.
Optimization
is when everyone is working
to help the company.*

*People care more for themselves
when they contribute to the
system.*

*People need to know
what their jobs are.*

Knowledge is the key.

Improve quality,
you automatically
improve productivity.

For Quality:
Stamp out fires, automate,
computerize, M.B.O.,
install merit pay, rank people,
best efforts, zero defects.
WRONG!!!
Missing ingredient:
profound knowledge.

*Best efforts will not
substitute
for knowledge.*

The customer
invents nothing.
New products and new services
come from the producer.

There is no substitute for knowledge.

*Quality starts
in the boardroom.*

There is no observation without theory.

The transformation can only be accomplished by man. A company cannot buy its way to quality.

*Management by results
is confusing
special causes with
common causes.*

A system must be managed.
It will not manage itself.

*You must have
a supplier relationship
of constant improvement.*

Build quality in.

There is nothing more costly than a hack.

We only have one chance,
only one!

*The process is not
just the sum of its parts.*

*It is so difficult to predict
the future.*

A goal without a method
is nonsense.

*Nobody
should try to use data
unless he has collected data.*

*It is easy to date
an earthquake,
but not an economic decline.*

*I am not reporting
things about people.
I am reporting
things about practices.*

Divide responsibility and nobody is responsible.

Could you do it yourself?
Do you have time to do it?
Why don't you?

*Without theory
there is nothing
to modify or learn.*

People are more interested in getting their money's worth than just buying American.

*Everyone is a customer
for somebody,
or a supplier
to somebody.*

*Any manager can do well
in an expanding market.*

*Manage the cause,
not the result.*

Without an aim,
there is no system.

*The product cannot
be made to perfection.*

*The most important figures
for management
of any organization
are unknown and unknowable.*

*Management's job
is to improve the system.*

Any two people have different ideas of what is important.

*They are just
doing their best.
How do they know?*

Without theory,
there are no questions.

The aim should be
to work on
the method of management.

There is very little evidence that we give a hoot about profit.

Are we noted for quality?

Lack of knowledge...
that is the problem.

Hold everybody accountable?
Ridiculous!

*The individual
has been crushed
by our style
of management today.*

A leader is a coach,
not a judge.

*Zero defects
is a super highway
going down the tube.*

*We can do something
about our problems or
continue the way we are.*

We know what we told him
but we don't know
what he heard.

*People are entitled
to joy in work.*

There will be quality of work life when people take pride in what they do.

It's management's job
to know.

Does experience help?
NO!
Not if we are doing the
wrong things.

Stamping out fires is a lot of fun, but it is only putting things back the way they were.

100% inspection will guarantee trouble.

Price is not the only cost.

*Every theory is correct
in its own world,
but the problem is that the
theory may not make contact
with this world.*

I met Mr. Murphy in London.
He is an optimist.

It only takes a little innovation.

*A leader knows
who is out of the system
and needs special help.*

*A rational prediction
has an explanation
based on theory.*

Management's job is to know which systems are stable and which are not.

A system is articulated activities directed toward an aim.

*You cannot plan
to make a discovery.
You do not plan innovation.*

All anyone asks for is a chance to work with pride.

The beginning of a system starts with the customer.

Without questions,
there is no learning.

Our problem is not the Japanese.

The biggest threat is at home.

*You can see from a flow diagram
who depends on you
and whom you can depend on.
You can now take joy
in your work.*

The result of long-term relationships is better and better quality, and lower and lower costs.

*Managing by results
is like looking in
the rear-view mirror.*

*If you stay in this world,
you will never learn
another one.*

You do not install quality;
you begin to work at it.

The problem is that most courses teach what is wrong.

People learn in different ways: reading, listening, pictures, watching.

*You only have one chance
to train a worker...
only one so don't muff it.*

The transformation will come from leadership.

We are being ruined
by the best efforts of people
who are doing the wrong
thing.

It is a mistake to assume that
if everybody does his job,
it will be all right.
The whole system may
be in trouble.

*Monetary rewards
are not a substitute
for intrinsic motivation.*

*Management's job is
to look ahead.*

*We should work on our processes,
not the outcome of our processes.*

We have to bring back the individual. Management has smothered the individual.

*The first line supervisor
has the devil's own job.*

*If you destroy the people of a company,
you do not have much left.*

*There is a penalty
for ignorance.
We are paying
through the nose.*